The Brighter Side of Darkness

Finding Light in the Depths of Depression

Anna Brown

All rights reserved. No part of this publication may be reproduced, distributed, or transmitted in any form or by any means, including photocopying, recording, or other electronic or mechanical methods, without the prior written permission of the publisher, except in the case of brief quotations embodied in critical reviews and certain other noncommercial uses permitted by copyright law.

TABLE OF CONTENTS

INTRODUCTION

The Importance of Mental Health

Your well-being greatly depends on your mental health. How you can function psychologically, emotionally, and socially, among other things, depends on this component of your wellness. Given the significant impact your mental health has on every element of your life, it is crucial to protect and enhance psychological well-being using the right strategies.

A person's ability to manage life's typical challenges is considered a sign of good mental health. This condition facilitates effective labor performance and allows for significant societal contributions. But there are other situations that could make it harder to deal with life's unexpected curveballs.

Daily activities and the ability to handle these changes may also be disrupted by these circumstances. A person's emotional, psychological, and social well-being are all aspects of their mental health. It is more significant since mental health issues have an impact on all elements of our lives and affect everything we do, think, and say. Both physical and mental health are essential to overall fitness. As an illustration, depression increases the risk of several physical health issues, particularly heart disease, diabetes, and stroke. The risk of mental disease can also be increased by chronic conditions. Maintaining a healthy mental state may increase productivity, improve our self-image, and strengthen our bonds with our loved ones. The following variables can have a detrimental impact on mental stability and health:

- Neglect, abuse, or past trauma
- Strong or persistent stress
- Isolation from others Loneliness
- Bereavement
- Discrimination
- Chronic physical ailments
- Societal limitations
- Poverty or substantial debt
- Unemployment
- Separation or divorce
- Unhealthy family dynamics

Although it is sometimes disregarded or misunderstood as being unimportant, mental health is an essential component of our general well-being. But in actuality, mental health is just as crucial to maintaining as physical health, and ignoring it may have negative effects on our lives. Positive mental moods and behaviors are also important components of mental health, in addition to the absence of mental disease.

The importance of mental health may be attributed to various factors. One reason is that our mental health has an impact on how we feel, think, and act every day. We are better equipped to handle stress, control our emotions, and make wise judgments when we have strong mental health. Additionally, we are more likely to enjoy life in general and have satisfying interpersonal interactions.

However, when our mental health is compromised, we may encounter several detrimental symptoms, such as anxiety, sadness, mood fluctuations, and difficulty focusing. These symptoms can make it difficult for us to go about our everyday lives and can have a variety of detrimental effects, including decreased productivity at work, strained relationships, and even physical health issues.

The possibility of negative effects on our communities and society at large is another factor in the significance of mental health. Increased rates of crime, substance misuse, and other societal problems can result when a big number of people experience mental health issues. Additionally, it may put stress on our healthcare system and raise prices. Given the significance of mental health, action must be taken to safeguard and advance it.

This might require a variety of tactics, including healthy self-care habits, getting help from a professional when necessary, and supporting laws that promote mental health. By doing this, we can make sure that we have the freedom to live our best lives and have a positive impact on society and our local communities.

CHAPTER ONE: UNDERSTANDING DEPRESSION

Symptoms of Depression

The medical issue of depression is complicated. It may have an impact on a person's whole life, including their personal relationships and physical health. Of course, it affects mental health. But being sad and being depressed is not the same thing.

The word "depression" is frequently used in a broad sense to describe how individuals feel through a breakup or after a difficult work week. Major depressive illness, sometimes referred to as clinical depression, is more than just a depressed mood.

Depression differs from the sort of broad melancholy that everyone occasionally feels by having specific symptoms. The signs of depression can be complicated and differ greatly from person to person.

You could experience sadness, hopelessness, and a loss of interest in once-enjoyable activities if you're depressed. The symptoms last for several weeks or months and are severe enough to affect your relationships with family, friends, and coworkers.

Psychological signs

Depression's psychological signs and symptoms include:

- Ongoing sorrow or depression
- Having no hope and being powerless
- A poor sense of self
- Emotion of tears
- Experiencing guilt
- Feeling agitated and intolerable toward other people
- Lacking enthusiasm or passion for tasks
- Finding it challenging to decide
- Not enjoying life to the fullest
- Feeling tense or concerned
- Possessing suicidal or self-destructive thoughts

Physical signs

Among the physical signs of depression are:

- Slowing down their movement or speech
- Changes in appetite or weight (often lower, but occasionally higher)
- Constipation
- Unaccounted for aches and discomfort

- Not enough energy
- Lack of libido and reduced sex desire
- Your menstrual cycle has changed
- Unrest in the sleep cycle, such as having trouble falling asleep at night or getting up too early in the morning

Social signs

Depression's social symptoms include:

- Avoiding friends' calls and participating in fewer social activities
- Ignoring your interests and pastimes
- Having issues with your family, job, or home life

Causes of Depression

What specifically causes depression is unknown. Many other causes might be at play, much like with many mental illnesses, including:

Biological variations: Genetics, environment, and life events are only a few of the many possible causes of depression, which is a complicated and diverse disorder. Biological variations are one element that has been demonstrated to contribute to depression. According to studies, those who have a family history of depression are more likely to have the disorder themselves, which raises the possibility that depression may have a genetic component.

However, it is still unclear exactly which genes are at play. It's crucial to remember that while genetics may contribute to sadness, it is seldom the only factor. Combinations of genetics, environment, and life events are frequently to blame for depression.

Brain chemistry: Neurotransmitters are organic brain substances that probably contribute to depression. According to recent studies, alterations in these neurotransmitters' effects and interactions with brain circuits involved in regulating mood stability may have a substantial impact on depression and its treatment. The various antidepressant drug classes may be useful in this situation.

Numerous antidepressants change the brain's levels of certain neurotransmitters. Serotonin is a neurotransmitter that can alter mood, and the most often prescribed type of antidepressant, known as SSRIs, blocks serotonin's reabsorption. The "serotonin hypothesis" postulated a connection between depression and low levels of this neurotransmitter. Serotonin levels were thought to rise, which would aid with mood enhancement and depression symptom relief.

Hormones: Depression may be brought on by or triggered by changes in the hormone balance in the body. Hormone shifts can occur during pregnancy, in the days or weeks following birth (postpartum), and as a result of thyroid issues, menopause, or a variety of other diseases.

Hormonal changes brought on by conditions like pregnancy, menopause, or birth control may change the neurotransmitters that influence mood. A decrease in hormones may cause serotonin levels to plummet, which may enhance feelings of melancholy, anxiety, and irritation. Reduced testosterone levels may also have an impact on mood, leading to despair and heightened anxiety.

Genetics: People with biological relations who also have this illness are more likely to experience depression. Researchers are looking for genes that could contribute to depression. According to some research, compared to the general population, someone who has a first-degree family (a parent, sibling, or child) who has been diagnosed with depression may be three times more likely to get the illness themselves. It is crucial to remember that while studies have shown a definite connection within families, these results do not take into account those who have depression without a familial history.

Types of Depression

Depression is a complex and multifaceted condition that can be caused by a wide range of factors, including genetics, environment, and life experiences. There are several different types of depression, each with its own unique symptoms and characteristics. While each type of depression is different, they all share the common trait of causing significant distress and impairment in daily life. There are several types of depression, including:

1. Major Depressive Disorder
2. Persistent Depressive Disorder
3. Seasonal Affective Disorder
4. Postpartum Depression
5. Bipolar Disorder

6. Psychotic Depression

Major Depressive Disorder

A mental health illness called major depressive disorder (MDD), commonly referred to as clinical depression, results in a consistently down or sad mood and a lack of interest in once-enjoyable activities. Additionally, clinical depression might impair your ability to think properly, eat, and sleep. It is a kind of depression that is distinguished by ongoing melancholy.

Some of the signs of MDD includes:

1. Changes in eating and sleep habits.
2. Difficulties focusing.
3. Feelings of shame or worthlessness.

For a diagnosis, these symptoms must be present for at least two weeks. These symptoms must not be caused by any medical or psychological illness and must be severe enough to interfere with everyday living. Although MDD is a chronic disorder, it often manifests in episodes that persist for a few weeks or months. More than one episode is likely to occur in your lifetime.

Contrary to mild or moderate depression that lasts for at least two years, persistent depressive illness is distinct.

MDD is a serious mental health illness that is prevalent and can have a big impact on everyday living. Psychotherapy, medicine, or a mix of the two are all possible forms of treatment for MDD. MDD is a condition that is effectively controlled with the right care.

Persistent Depressive Disorder

A persistent, protracted type of depression is known as persistent depressive disorder. You can experience melancholy and emptiness, lose interest in routine tasks, and struggle to complete them. You could also experience poor self-esteem, failure, and hopelessness.

These emotions might persist for years and can get in the way of your relationships, studies, job, and everyday routine. Even in pleasant moments, it could be difficult for someone with a chronic depressive illness to feel positive.

You can be characterized as having a depressing disposition, groaning all the time, or lacking the ability to have fun. The severity of your present sad mood may be mild, moderate, or severe, although persistent depressive illness is not as bad as major depression. Symptoms of persistent depressive illness typically appear and disappear over several years. Over time, symptoms' severity might vary.

However, symptoms typically last for longer than two months at a time. Major depressive episodes can also happen before or during persistent depressive illness.

Signs of Persistent Depressive Disorder include:
1. Sadness, emptiness, or a depressed mood.
2. A decline in interest in routine tasks.
3. Fatigue and little energy.
4. Low self-esteem, self-criticism, or a sense of inadequacy.
5. Having problems concentrating and making judgments.
6. Difficulties doing tasks effectively and on schedule.
7. Being quickly irritated, irritable, or furious.
8. Avoiding social interactions.
9. Guilt-ridden thoughts and concerns about the past.
10. Overeating or a poor appetite.
11. Sleep issues.
12. Hopelessness.

Dealing with depression symptoms might be difficult due to the persistent depressive disorder's duration. Treatment for this illness may involve both medication and talk therapy.

Seasonal Affective Disorder

A kind of sadness known as seasonal affective disorder (SAD) is triggered by the changing of the seasons; it starts and ends at about the same periods each year. Since there is less sunshine throughout the fall and winter, it generally happens during those seasons.

SAD symptoms include:
1. Sadness and a sense of helplessness
2. Fatigue
3. Alterations in appetite
4. Alterations in sleeping habits
5. Difficulty paying attention
6. Loss of interest in once-enjoyable activities

Even though the precise origin of SAD is unknown, it is thought to be connected to alterations in the body's circadian rhythms and the synthesis of melatonin, a hormone that controls sleep. Your symptoms, which drain your energy and make you cranky, likely begin in the fall for the majority of individuals and last throughout the winter.

Typically, these symptoms go away in the spring and summer. Light therapy (phototherapy), which includes exposing patients to intense light for a certain period each day, is one possible kind of treatment. Psychotherapy, medicine, or a mix of the two are examples of additional therapies.

Postpartum Depression

Having a child transforms your life. Parenting is fun, but it can also be exhausting and overwhelming. It's common to feel anxious or unsure, particularly if you're a first-time parent.

However, you could develop postpartum depression if your emotions include excessive melancholy or loneliness, wild mood fluctuations, and a lot of weeping.

Depression that follows childbirth is known as postpartum depression (PPD). Not just the individual giving birth is impacted by postpartum depression. Adoptive parents and surrogates are also susceptible. After having a kid, people go through hormonal, physical, emotional, monetary, and social changes. Postpartum depression symptoms may be brought on by these changes.

Some people experience embarrassment over their symptoms or believe they are bad parents for having such feelings. Postpartum depression is quite prevalent. It doesn't make you a horrible person; you're not the only one who feels this way.

If you go through any of the following, you may be suffering from postpartum depression:

1. Sadness, worthlessness, hopelessness, or guilt.
2. Overly fretting or being tense.
3. Loss of interest in past interests or pastimes.
4. Appetite changes or not eating.
5. Loss of motivation and energy.
6. Having trouble falling asleep or always wanting to sleep.
7. Crying excessively or without cause.
8. Thinking or concentration challenges.
9. Suicidal ideas or wishes to pass away.
10. Lack of interest in your child or unease around your child.

11. Intrusive thoughts of harming your child or feelings of dissatisfaction with having a child.

Bipolar Disorder

Extreme mood fluctuations, including emotional highs (mania or hypomania) and lows (depression), are symptoms of bipolar illness, formerly known as manic depression. When you experience depression, you could feel melancholy or hopeless and stop enjoying or being interested in most things.

You could experience mania or hypomania (a less severe form of mania), which can make you feel elated, energized, or particularly irritated. The capacity to think, energy levels, activity, judgment, and behavior can all be impacted by these mood changes. Mood swing episodes might happen seldom or repeatedly each year.

While the majority of people will have some emotional symptoms in between bouts, some people might not. Although bipolar illness is a lifelong diagnosis, by adhering to a treatment plan, you can control your mood swings and other symptoms. Bipolar illness is often treated with pharmaceuticals, psychotherapy, and dietary modifications.

Depending on the kind of episode (manic, hypomanic, or depressed), bipolar disorder symptoms might change.

Among the signs of a manic episode are:
1. Feeling euphoric or excessively cheerful.
2. Being highly energized and restless.
3. Rapid-fire speech and rushing thoughts

Among the signs of a hypomanic episode are:
1. Feeling incredibly motivated and productive.
2. Having an unusually creative feeling
3. More talking than normal

Among the signs of a depressive episode are:
1. Feeling depressed or hopeless
2. Losing interest in once-enjoyable activities
3. Having difficulty sleeping or sleeping excessively
4. Feeling worn out or low in energy
5. Having trouble focusing or choosing things
6. Guilt or worthlessness
7. Having suicidal or self-destructive thoughts.

Psychotic Depression

When a severe depressive disease involves some degree of psychosis, a subtype of major depression known as psychotic depression develops.

Hallucinations (such as hearing a voice telling you that you are no good or worthless), delusions (such as having strong emotions of failure, unworthiness, or having committed a sin), or other dissociation from reality might all be symptoms of psychosis.

One in every four patients with depression who are hospitalized also has psychotic depression. Hallucinations and delusions are some of the psychotic symptoms that define it.

Among the signs of psychotic depression are:
1. Sad or despairing feelings.
2. Having difficulty sleeping or sleeping excessively.
3. Feeling worn out or low in energy.
4. Having trouble staying focused.
5. Having hallucinations, which include hearing voices or seeing things that aren't there.

6. Having delusions, which include thinking that someone is trying to harm you or that you are suffering from a terrible illness.

Treatment for psychotic depression should start right away. Medication, psychotherapy, or a combination of the two may be used to treat psychotic depression.

CHAPTER TWO: THE IMPACT OF DEPRESSION

The Physical Effects of Depression

While depression is often thought of as a mental health condition, it can also affect the body in a number of ways.

Fatigue

Fatigue is among the most typical physical side effects of depression. Even after a full night of sleep, people with depression may feel worn out or fatigued. This exhaustion may make it challenging to do everyday duties and may negatively affect employment or academic performance. There are several ways that depression might make you feel tired.

Modifying sleep habits is one method. People who struggle with depression may have difficulty getting asleep or staying asleep, which can result in daytime fatigue and weariness.

Additionally, depressive disorders can alter the brain's levels of neurotransmitters like serotonin and norepinephrine, which can also heighten the sense of exhaustion. Fatigue may also result from physical changes brought on by depression in the body. For instance, depression can result in changes in appetite and weight, which can exacerbate tiredness.

Additionally, depression can affect the immune system, increasing a person's susceptibility to diseases and infections as well as their sense of exhaustion. Finally, depression can cause alterations in how a person experiences and perceives their environment. People who are depressed may see life negatively and feel helpless or hopeless. These emotions could deplete you and make you feel exhausted.

Overall, depression may lead to exhaustion in a variety of ways, including physical changes in the body and adjustments in how people view and interact with their environment. To alleviate the condition's mental and physical symptoms, persons with depression must get help from a mental health specialist.

Changes in appetite and weight

Weight and appetite changes might result from depression. When depressed, some people may have decreased appetites and lose weight, while others may have increased appetites and put on weight.

These weight fluctuations may further exacerbate poor self-esteem and a negative body image. Numerous factors, including depression, can influence changes in appetite and weight. One method involves alterations in the concentrations of certain neurotransmitters in the brain, such as serotonin and norepinephrine, which can impact metabolism and hunger.

People who are depressed may lose weight when their hunger decreases or gain weight when their appetite increases. A person's perception and experience of eating may also change as a result of depression. People who are depressed may use food as a coping mechanism for unpleasant feelings, which can result in overeating and weight gain.

Alternately, those who are depressed may completely lose interest in food, which can result in undereating and weight loss. The body's hormone levels, including those of cortisol, which regulates metabolism and hunger, might vary as a result of depression.

For instance, high cortisol levels can cause an increase in hunger and weight gain, whereas low cortisol levels might cause an appetite drop and weight loss. And last, depression can affect how a person feels about and experiences their body. Negative body image is common in people with depression, and it can lead to disordered eating habits and weight fluctuations.

Overall, sadness may affect hunger and weight in a variety of ways, including physical changes to the body and mental shifts in how individuals view and relate to food and their bodies. In order to alleviate the condition's mental and physical symptoms, it's critical for persons with depression to get help from a mental health specialist.

Immune system deficiency
Depression can affect the immune system as well. People who are depressed may be more prone to infections and diseases, and they may recover from sickness more slowly.

Furthermore, depression has been related to chronic inflammation, which has been connected to a variety of health issues such as heart disease, diabetes, and cancer.

Depression can suppress the immune system, increasing the likelihood of getting certain diseases and health issues. When a person is sad, their body produces more stress chemicals like cortisol and adrenaline. These hormones have the potential to inhibit the immune system's ability to combat infections and illnesses.

Furthermore, depression can impair the body's synthesis of cytokines, which are proteins that aid in the regulation of the immune response. When cytokine production is disturbed, inflammation and other immune system abnormalities can occur. These immune system inadequacies, over time, can raise the chance of acquiring a variety of health issues such as infections, autoimmune diseases, and some forms of cancer.

It is crucial to highlight that depression is a complicated disorder with several causes and contributing variables, and the link between depression and the immune system is currently poorly understood.

Cardiovascular system deficiency

Finally, depression can affect the cardiovascular system. People who are depressed may have a higher risk of heart disease and stroke, as well as changes in heart rate and blood pressure.

Depression has been related to an increased risk of cardiovascular disease, which can result in a variety of health issues including heart attacks, strokes, and heart failure.

Depression can exacerbate cardiovascular system inadequacies by raising inflammation in the body. When a person is sad, their body produces more stress chemicals like cortisol and adrenaline, which can cause chronic inflammation.

This inflammation, over time, can damage blood vessels and raise the risk of developing cardiovascular disease. Depression can also increase the chance of other risk factors for cardiovascular disease, such as high blood pressure, high cholesterol, and obesity.

Depressed people are less likely to participate in healthy behaviors such as exercise and good eating, which can raise their risk of cardiovascular disease.

The Emotional Effects of Depression

Depression may have a variety of emotional impacts on a person's mood, thoughts, and behaviors. The following are some of the most prevalent emotional repercussions of depression:

Feelings of sorrow or hopelessness

Depression can result in a lingering sensation of melancholy or despair that makes it challenging to find joy or pleasure in things that were formerly pleasurable.

Due to alterations in brain chemistry and activity, depression can lead to emotions of melancholy or hopelessness. Serotonin and dopamine levels in the brain can be affected by a variety of genetic, environmental, and biological variables, which are considered to contribute to depression.

When these chemicals—which are in charge of controlling mood—are out of balance, it can result in depressive symptoms like despair and sorrow.

Additionally, depression may alter how the brain functions, which may affect how a person interprets their feelings and experiences. This might make it challenging to appreciate things that were formerly fun and can result in a lingering sense of melancholy or pessimism.

Sleep disturbances

Changes in sleep habits, such as insomnia or oversleeping, can be brought on by depression. Sleep habits and emotional health can be significantly impacted by depression for the person experiencing it.

Feelings of sorrow, despair, and anxiety brought on by depression can make it challenging to get to sleep and maintain sleep.

Furthermore, sadness can result in a lingering sensation of exhaustion or low energy, which can make it challenging to remain awake and aware throughout the day.

Depression-related sleep disruptions can be detrimental to one's emotional health. For instance, lack of sleep might result in irritation, mood fluctuations, and difficulties focusing.

A chronic sensation of exhaustion or low energy may also be brought on by sleep disruptions, which can make it challenging to participate in activities or interact socially. Feelings of seclusion, loneliness, and melancholy may result from this.

Difficulty concentrating

Depression can affect a person's ability to concentrate or make decisions, which might affect how well they do at a job or in school. There are several ways that depression may make it difficult to focus.

First of all, sadness can result in a lingering sensation of exhaustion or low energy, which makes it challenging to remain attentive and concentrated. Furthermore, depression can result in emotions like sorrow, helplessness, and worry that can be distracting and make it challenging to focus on activities.

Changes in brain chemistry that impact cognitive performance can also be brought on by depression. For instance, depression can result in a reduction in the synthesis of certain neurotransmitters that are important for controlling mood and cognitive function, such as serotonin and norepinephrine.

This may result in symptoms including trouble focusing, memory issues, and low motivation. The structure and operation of the brain can also alter as a result of depression. For instance, depression can result in a reduction in the size of the hippocampus, a region of the brain important for memory and learning. Problems with memory and focus may result from this.

Irritability or anger

Relationships with loved ones might be strained by the impatience or hostility that depression can bring on. Millions of individuals throughout the world suffer from a dangerous mental health disorder known as depression. A variety of symptoms, such as impatience and rage, might result from it.

A depressed individual could feel emotionally overburdened, which might make them lash out at other people. The brain's capacity to control emotions is one of the main ways depression can lead to irritation and rage.

A depressed person's changed brain chemistry might make it challenging for them to manage their emotions. They could be more quickly angered or frustrated because they may feel more sensitive to stimuli.

Depression can result in emotions of helplessness and hopelessness, which can also make a person irritable and angry. When someone is depressed, they could believe that they have little control over their lives, which can lead to feelings of rage or resentment. Additionally, they could feel like a burden, which might make them snap at others around them.

The Social Effects of Depression

Depression can also have a range of social effects, which can impact a person's relationships, work, and overall quality of life. Some common social effects of depression include:

Isolation

Depression can cause a person to feel alone or cut off from others, which can cause social withdrawal and make it difficult to sustain connections. The first thing you should not do when depressed is frequently what you end up doing.

While it is simple to get isolated while depressed, maintaining connections is essential. Depression not only makes you feel alone, but it also makes you want to be alone. The symptoms of depression, such as anxiety, altered eating and sleeping patterns, feelings of worthlessness, a lack of interest in daily activities, and suicidal thoughts, can be made worse by social isolation, which in turn can exacerbate depression.

A physiological demand for social interaction exists in humans. You start to experience a loss of connection, support, and sense of belonging when that need is ignored. Depression has an isolating effect that prevents you from hearing compliments from others.

You are the only one who can hear. Typically, depressed individuals don't think well of themselves. However, when you isolate yourself from others, you have plenty of time to tell yourself unfavorable things.

Financial problems

Depression can cause a person to feel alone or cut off from others, which can cause social withdrawal and make it difficult to sustain connections. The first thing you should not do when depressed is frequently what you end up doing. While it is simple to get isolated while depressed, maintaining connections is essential.

Depression not only makes you feel alone, but it also makes you want to be alone. The symptoms of depression, such as anxiety, altered eating and sleeping patterns, feelings of worthlessness, a lack of interest in daily activities, and suicidal thoughts, can be made worse by social isolation, which in turn can exacerbate depression.

A physiological demand for social interaction exists in humans. You start to experience a loss of connection, support, and sense of belonging when that need is ignored. Depression has an isolating effect that prevents you from hearing compliments from others. You are the only one who can hear. Typically, depressed individuals don't think well of themselves. However, when you isolate yourself from others, you have plenty of time to tell yourself unfavorable things.

Relationship problems

Relationships with loved ones may suffer due to depression, which can cause conflict and poor communication. Peeling back the layers of sadness reveals that it's not just one major issue; rather, it's the tiny things that stack up and weigh you down day after day.

This is due to the self-derating loop that melancholy and stress induce, which affects how you see everything in life, including your relationship. It's no secret that partnerships provide us with a variety of challenges. We become more vulnerable in relationships as we try to build mutual trust.

However, these difficulties can become more severe and lead to vulnerability and mistrust when a partner in a relationship has depression. While it's normal for individuals to have to work out issues and adjust to one another's sensitivities in a new relationship, depression can bring up issues and sensitivities that are intense, unexpected, and occasionally resistant to resolution.

Contrary to certain common misconceptions about depression, a person who is clinically sad can nevertheless enjoy their relationship. That's because depression is a severe mental disorder that may hurt your relationships and health. It's more than just feeling sad or having a terrible day.

Unfortunately, the loneliness and isolation brought on by melancholy may damage any relationship. It may be incredibly unpleasant for two individuals in a relationship when a depressed person exhibits crippling tiredness and hopelessness. Depression can not fit one mold since every person experiences it differently. Depression can manifest itself in a variety of ways. People may experience shame, worthlessness, fatigue, and anxiety as a result. An unbroken loop of self-destructive actions that eventually destroy relationships can result from untreated depression.

Substance abuse

To deal with their symptoms, depressed people may turn to drugs or alcohol, which can result in substance misuse issues. Millions of individuals all over the world suffer from the mental health condition of depression. It can result in a variety of symptoms, such as depression, hopelessness, and despair.

Unfortunately, a lot of individuals who are depressed turn to drinking or drugs to help them deal with their feelings. This can result in drug misuse, which might have detrimental effects on someone's health and well-being. People may use drugs or alcohol as self-medication for depression, which is one of the reasons why depression can result in substance misuse.

They could believe that the only way to deal with their emotions of melancholy or hopelessness is to use drugs or alcohol. Sadly, this can result in a vicious cycle of reliance when a person becomes dependent on drink or drugs to feel better. Depression may alter a person's brain chemistry, which is another factor why it might result in substance misuse. Because depression alters the chemistry of the brain, it might increase a person's susceptibility to addiction.

Additionally, they could feel stronger cravings for drugs or alcohol, which can make it challenging for them to stop. It's crucial to keep in mind that substance misuse is a disorder that can be treated, and there are several efficient therapies accessible.

Stigma

The stigma and prejudice that some people with depression may face might make it challenging for them to get care or discuss their condition. Millions of individuals all over the world suffer from the mental health condition of depression. Sadly, there is still a lot of stigma associated with depression, which makes it challenging for people to get assistance.

People who experience stigma may also feel humiliated or embarrassed about their disease, which makes it more difficult for them to discuss it with others. Because many people still think that mental health issues are a sign of weakness, depression can still be stigmatized.

People may be reluctant to seek assistance as a result of this, which can make them feel ashamed or embarrassed about their illness. People who experience stigma may also feel isolated in their challenges, which makes it more difficult for them to express their emotions to others. People may not understand depression, which is another factor that contributes to stigma.

They could believe that depression is only a sad emotion that can be fought off with resolve. This can make individuals disregard those who are dealing with depression, which makes it more difficult for them to open out and get assistance.

CHAPTER THREE: SEEKING HELP

Recognizing the Need for Help

An essential first step in treating mental health issues like depression is admitting that you need help. Although admitting that you need help might be challenging, doing so can be the first step toward getting better. There are various indications that you could require depression treatment.

The most typical symptoms include persistent feelings of sadness or hopelessness, losing interest in past interests, suffering changes in eating or sleep habits, and feeling worn out or low on energy. Additionally, you could discover that you're having trouble focusing or making judgments, as well as that you're feeling agitated or restless.

It is crucial to express your feelings to someone if you're going through any of these signs. This may be a friend, relative, or mental health specialist.

It is critical to keep in mind that many individuals have mental health issues at some time in their life and that asking for help is a show of strength, not weakness. You have a wide range of alternatives while seeking depression treatment. You might want to start by speaking with your primary care physician, who can advise you on treatment choices and assist you in determining whether you have depression.

You could also think about consulting a mental health expert, such a therapist or psychiatrist, who can help you manage your symptoms with therapy or medication.

Support groups are one of the additional possibilities for assistance since they may offer a secure and encouraging atmosphere for individuals with depression to share their experiences and learn from others.

Consider self-help techniques that can help you control your symptoms and feel better, such exercise, meditation, or journaling. In conclusion, the first step in treating depression is realizing that you need support.

Medications for Depression

Prescription drugs called antidepressants are used to treat depression. They are also prescribed by medical professionals to treat various diseases. One method of therapy for depression is antidepressants. While they help alleviate depression's symptoms, they don't always deal with its root causes.

This is why medical professionals frequently suggest psychotherapy (talk therapy) in conjunction with antidepressants. In the 1950s, antidepressants were developed. Since then, scientists have created other variants of the drug.

Antidepressants are currently one of the most often prescribed drugs in the US. Antidepressants often alter how your brain uses specific chemicals (referred to as neurotransmitters) to better control your mood and behavior.

They specifically influence serotonin, norepinephrine, and, less frequently, dopamine-related neurotransmission. To do this, various antidepressants all function in various ways.

Additionally, research indicates that antidepressants promote neuroplasticity, a process through which your brain may change the way it is organized by tightening or loosening connections between its neurons.

The most common type of antidepressant is a pill (tablet). The tablets are taken with a beverage, such as water. Your doctor will likely recommend the lowest dose of the antidepressant they believe is required to alleviate your symptoms when you first start taking it. They will change the dosage as needed over time. Before you begin to notice an improvement in your symptoms, it may take many weeks.

After you start to feel better, treatment typically lasts at least six months. Your healthcare professional could suggest taking the antidepressant for the foreseeable future if you suffer from recurring, chronic, or severe depression. The best drug for treating the signs and symptoms of depression is an antidepressant.

Antidepressants may, however, benefit some individuals more than others, much like many other drugs. According to studies, the benefit of taking an antidepressant is often correlated with how bad the depression is; the worse the depression, the higher the benefit or "effectiveness" will be.

In cases of mild, moderately severe, or chronic depression, antidepressants are typically beneficial. They frequently don't alleviate minor depression. It's crucial to keep in mind that psychotherapy is a crucial component of depression treatment.
The most improvement in your symptoms will often be seen when you combine psychotherapy and depression medication.

There are several potential adverse effects for each kind (class) of antidepressant and each brand. It's crucial to discuss any potential side effects of the specific drug you're taking or considering taking with your doctor or pharmacist.

Antidepressants frequently cause the following negative effects, in general:

1. Stomach pains.
2. Diarrhea.
3. Headache.
4. Drowsiness.
5. Sexual dysfunction

Antidepressant types
Selective Serotonin Reuptake Inhibitors
In the middle to late 1980s, selective serotonin reuptake inhibitors (SSRIs) were introduced. The most popular class of antidepressants used to treat depression is now this generation.

Citalopram, escitalopram, paroxetine, fluoxetine, and sertraline are a few examples. Vilazodone and vortioxetine are two medications that are categorized as "serotonin modulators and stimulators" or SMSs (meaning they have some comparable features to SSRIs but also activate other brain receptors).

Although most side effects are minor, some people may find them unpleasant. They consist of headaches, nausea, stomach discomfort, sexual issues, exhaustion, wooziness, and sleeplessness.

Serotonin and Norepinephrine Reuptake Inhibitor

A more recent kind of antidepressant is known as a serotonin and norepinephrine reuptake inhibitor (SNRI). Venlafaxine, desvenlafaxine, duloxetine, and levomilnacipran are all members of this class. Side effects might include nausea, sleeplessness, erectile dysfunction, anxiety, vertigo, and exhaustion.

Tricyclic Antidepressants

One of the first drugs used to treat depression was a class of drugs known as tricyclic antidepressants (TCAs). Amitriptyline, Desipramine, Doxepin, Amitriptyline, Nortriptyline, Protriptyline, and Trimipramine are a few examples. Consequences might include nausea, vomiting, dry mouth, changes in blood pressure and blood sugar levels, and stomach distress.

Monoamine Oxidase Inhibitors

One of the first medications for treating depression was called a monoamine oxidase inhibitor (MAOI). Monoamine oxidase, an enzyme that the MAOIs inhibit, leads to an increase in mood-related brain chemicals including serotonin, norepinephrine, and dopamine.

Examples include transdermal selegiline (the EMSAM skin patch), phenelzine, tranylcypromine, isocarboxazid, and other drugs.

Despite their effectiveness, MAOIs are not frequently administered due to the possibility of dangerous interactions with several other drugs and certain foods. Aged cheese and aged meats are foods that can interact poorly with MAOIs.

Other drugs include:
Bupropion
The brain chemicals norepinephrine and dopamine are hypothesized to be affected by the special antidepressant bupropion. The majority of the time, side effects are minor and include nausea, headaches, sleeplessness, and anxiety.

Compared to other antidepressants, bupropion may have a lower risk of having negative sexual side effects.

Esketamine

Esketamine is a special drug that was first created as an anesthetic and is believed to treat depression despite having an impact on the glutamate molecule in the brain. It is used for those who have not responded to therapy with conventional antidepressants and is given as a nasal spray.

Sedation, dissociation (having unusual time- and space perceptions or feeling as if everything around you is not real), cognitive difficulties, and elevated blood pressure are some of its most frequent adverse effects. If any of these negative effects do manifest, they are often minor and transient.

Mirtazapine

Another distinct antidepressant is mirtazapine, which is hypothesized to primarily influence serotonin and norepinephrine through distinct brain receptors from other medications.

Because it frequently makes people drowsy, it is typically given before night. Sleepiness, weight gain, increased triglycerides, and dizziness are among the milder side effects.

Trazodone

The standard way to take trazodone is with meals to lower the risk of gastrointestinal discomfort. Drowsiness, wooziness, diarrhea, dry tongue, and blurred vision are further adverse effects.It is frequently recommended as a sleep aid.

Tips on how to maximize the effects of depression medication

1. Watch your mood.
2. Boost your network of support
3. Follow the recommended course of action
4. Consult a depression specialist
5. Create virtuous behaviors
6. Don't disregard adverse consequences
7. If another medical expert has prescribed you medication, inform your doctor.
8. Never stop taking depression medication without consulting your doctor.

9. Don't think that once you feel better, you can stop taking your medication for depression.

Therapy for Depression

Treatments for depression and other mood disorders come in a wide variety of forms.

Since psychotherapy may assist you in exploring the underlying causes of your sad symptoms and teaching you new coping mechanisms, it can be an effective type of treatment for depression.

The intensity of your symptoms, your personal preferences, and your treatment objectives will all play a role in determining the ideal style of psychotherapy for you.

There is evidence to support the effectiveness of the therapy techniques listed below in treating depression.

How Does Psychotherapy Work?

The process of treating psychological illnesses with psychological and linguistic methods is known as psychotherapy.

To assist people to recognize and change unfavorable thinking or behavioral patterns, the majority of psychotherapy techniques encourage a therapeutic alliance between the therapist and the client.

Psychotherapy is sometimes referred to as "talk therapy" since it entails a patient and a psychotherapist conversing while they are both seated in a room. However, it goes much beyond that.

Psychotherapists have received professional training in several strategies that they use to assist clients in overcoming mental illness, resolving interpersonal conflicts, and making good life changes. No one strategy works for everyone, and the best kind of therapy for depression relies on several different variables.

Your preferences and the intensity of your symptoms, among other things, may influence the sort of treatment you select. To help you choose the sort of therapy that could be best for you, have a look at some of the following often-used forms of treatment for depression.

Cognitive Therapy

The fundamental tenet of cognitive therapy is that our ideas may influence our feelings. For instance, we will be more likely to feel happy if we choose to search for the positive in every event rather than the negative.

Depressive disorders can be exacerbated and influenced by negative thinking. When you're mired in a stream of unfavorable ideas, feeling happy is difficult.

Cognitive therapy teaches patients how to spot typical cognitive distortions, which are negative thought patterns that may be changed into more uplifting ones to elevate mood.

Goals are generally the focus of short-term cognitive therapy. There is "homework" practice to complete outside of treatment, and therapy sessions are scheduled with a defined agenda for each session. The typical duration of cognitive treatment is six weeks to four months.

Behavioral Therapy

Behavioral therapy is focused on altering actions that impact emotions rather than the negative ideas that lead to depression which is the focus of cognitive therapy.

Behavioral activation is a key component of behavioral therapy for depression. This involves encouraging patients to take part in activities that will improve their sense of well-being.

Cognitive-Behavioral Therapy

Cognitive behavioral therapy (CBT) is a treatment strategy that frequently combines cognitive therapy and behavioral therapy because it effectively treats depression and anxiety disorders. The primary goal of CBT is to change both the harmful cognitive patterns and the harmful actions that lead to depression.

Your therapist could advise you to keep a notebook to record the week's events and any self-defeating or depressing responses to them.

One pattern of thought you could work on during CBT is automatic negative reactions, often known as habitual negative reactions to situations. Overgeneralization and all-or-nothing thinking, two typical cognitive distortions, are examples of additional reaction patterns.

Once you can identify your reaction patterns, your therapist will help you develop new ways of thinking and acting.

Additionally, work on using constructive self-talk. CBT is often succinct and goal-oriented, just like cognitive therapy and behavioral therapy. It often entails five to twenty scheduled sessions that are devoted to resolving particular issues.

As "homework," CBT sessions frequently involve journaling, practicing relaxation techniques, doing readings, and using worksheets with predetermined objectives.

According to research, CBT can be helpful in the treatment of depression and may have long-lasting benefits that shield patients from experiencing depressed symptoms again in the future.

Dialectical Behavior Therapy

The main foundation of dialectical behavior therapy is CBT. It requires people with depression to admit and accept their bad thoughts and behaviors, which is the main distinction.

Individuals may learn to deal with their negative emotions, control their reactions to stress, and even enhance their relationships with others via the practice of validation.

In this kind of psychotherapy, crisis coaching—in which a person can call the therapist for advice on how to face trying circumstances—also combines mindfulness techniques from Buddhist traditions.

The person will soon be more capable of handling their difficult situations on their own as they continue to practice these new abilities.

Psychodynamic Counseling

Psychodynamic treatment, commonly referred to as psychoanalytic therapy, assumes that unresolved conflicts, typically unconscious conflicts that date back to infancy, can lead to depression.

The objectives of this sort of treatment are to assist the patient in better tolerating these sentiments and putting them in a helpful context, as well as to help the patient become more conscious of their whole spectrum of emotions, including contradicting and difficult ones.

Contrary to several other depression treatment modalities, psychodynamic therapy is typically more prolonged and less targeted. This method can help make connections between earlier experiences and determine how those experiences may have influenced how depressed you felt. Additionally, this method can improve specific emotional skills and self-awareness.

Interpersonal Therapy
Depression-related sentiments can also be influenced by interpersonal conflict and a lack of social support. An approach to treatment called interpersonal therapy focuses on these problems by talking about interpersonal relationships and social roles from the past and present.

The therapist often selects one or two issue areas to concentrate on during therapy. This sort of treatment often lasts only a few sessions and focuses on your social interactions with significant others. Relationships with your spouse, friends, family, and coworkers are examples of this.

To practice and enhance your communication, your therapist may urge you to role-play various scenarios. The idea is that by doing this, you will be able to apply these tactics in your relationships and create a more robust network of social support.

Alternative Treatments for Depression

Alternative, complementary, or integrative are terms used to describe medical procedures that are not considered to be part of conventional Western medical practice. An alternative treatment involves a wide range of disciplines, including everything from your nutrition and exercise routine to your lifestyle and mental preparation.

Although no alternative therapy can promise to cure depression, many Western medications and psychotherapies also lack this assurance. be safe, and make sure you speak with your doctor before doing any of these suggested treatments. Every alternative treatment is special. Some require motion, some require stillness, etc. Each treatment operates as follows:

Acupuncture: Acupuncture involves inserting very small, firm needles into particular body locations. Addressing imbalances, it increases the body's capacity to fight off or recover from sickness. Additionally, it causes the body to create molecules that lessen or completely get rid of unpleasant sensations.

Reflexology: Different bodily parts are connected to the nerves in the hands and feet. According to reflexologists, pressing on particular body locations might encourage the healing process.

Exercise: Exercise has been demonstrated to lessen the symptoms of depression. Examples include walking, jogging, swimming, etc. According to a new study, 150 minutes per week of moderate-intensity exercise can lessen depressive and anxious symptoms.

Meditation: By concentrating on a single thought—which may be a word, a phrase, or a specific scene—while the body is at rest, the mind is cleaned. Most people consistently meditate for at least 10 minutes each day.

Massage: Massage therapists touch your body with their hands. By fostering the mind-body connection, massage enhances our awareness of how our bodies are functioning. Swedish massage methods, Reiki, aromatherapy, and craniosacral treatments are a few types of massage that can enhance the mind-body connection and overall relaxation.

Guided imagery: With the help of a coach, you may train your mind to conjure up relaxing, tranquil pictures as a "mental escape" for therapeutic purposes. Enhancing a person's coping abilities can be a potent psychological tactic.

Yoga: When you do yoga, you learn breathing methods that can help you feel more upbeat when you're feeling sad or tranquil when you're feeling anxious. Your mind and body are connected through your breath. You can feel better both physically and psychologically by changing the way you breathe.

Deep Breathing: When we're under pressure, we frequently breathe quickly or find it difficult to catch our breath. Your lungs will fill with oxygen when you inhale slowly and deeply, which will assist to calm down your heartbeat. We may turn our attention away from the source of the tension by concentrating on the act of breathing.

CHAPTER FOUR: COPING STRATEGIES

Managing Symptoms of Depression

The process of controlling depression's symptoms can be difficult and continual.

However, several methods and remedies can enhance your quality of life and help you feel better. Therapy is among the most efficient approaches to treating depression.

You can learn coping mechanisms to control your symptoms and the underlying reasons for your depression with the aid of therapy.

There are several varieties of therapy, such as cognitive-behavioral therapy, which focuses on altering unhelpful thought processes, and interpersonal therapy, which focuses on enhancing interpersonal connections.

Medication can be a successful treatment for depression in addition to counseling. Antidepressant drugs can assist in regulating the brain chemicals that influence mood and can be used in conjunction with treatment to treat symptoms. Altering one's way of life can also help manage depression.

Exercise has been demonstrated to be very helpful in elevating mood and easing depressive symptoms. Additionally, a good diet and sufficient sleep might help you feel better and have fewer symptoms.

Other methods for treating depression include learning relaxation techniques like meditation or deep breathing, as well as taking part in enjoyable activities like hobbies or socializing with loved ones.

It is crucial to keep in mind that controlling depression is a continuous process and that it could take some time to discover the optimal therapy combination for you.

Additionally, it's critical to get treatment if you're showing signs of depression because early intervention can enhance results and lower the likelihood of problems.

In conclusion, treating depression-related symptoms calls for a multifaceted strategy that combines counseling, medication, lifestyle modifications, and other tactics. People with depression may control their symptoms and lead satisfying lives with the correct support and care.

Developing Coping Skills

The first step to recovering from depression or a gloomy mood is admitting that you are going through it. It implies that your symptoms are not being ignored. You're conscious that you require assistance, and you want to take action.

These coping techniques were developed with the aid of research and a depression specialist.

Give yourself enough time to do them. If some of these work for you, fantastic! Keep applying them. If some don't, put them on hold and try again later.

Perform one act of self-care.
Maintaining a regular schedule is one of the toughest things to accomplish when you're sad. You might not always feel like taking a shower, cleaning your teeth, or donning clean clothing. Simply choose one self-care activity to engage in if you are experiencing this. Just getting dressed or taking a shower might improve your attitude.

Consult your network of supporters
When you're sad, you could feel like a burden to other people, but that's probably just the depression talking. Just

as you would want to be there for them if the positions were reversed, your friends and family want to support you.

According to research, talking to trustworthy family members rather than isolating oneself when you're sad might be more beneficial. Try a phone call or video chat if you don't feel like going out or having someone around. It could tide you over until you're prepared to interact with others face-to-face.

Exercise.

Exercise naturally elevates your mood. If you're experiencing emotional paralysis or a sense of being stuck, consider taking a little stroll outside. If venturing outside seems like too much, pace about your living room or stand still in front of the TV while listening to your favorite music. A little exercise may make a big difference in your ability to feel better.

Examine different snack choices

Did you realize that certain meals might impact how you feel?For instance, eating sugary foods and beverages might make depression symptoms worse. Additionally, the caffeine in sodas and coffee might make people feel more anxious.

You can use food as a coping mechanism since it might affect your emotions. Consider eating something that will sate your desires without making you feel bad.

Transform it into a test. How many different meals can you attempt? What fresh flavors can you find? Your mood can be impacted by eating habits including missing meals and having a little appetite.

In fact, research raises the possibility that missing breakfast and depression levels are related. Therefore, remember to eat throughout the day at regular intervals.

Keep a thinking journal.
Sometimes, negative thoughts might make your depression symptoms worse. Write down your ideas and scan them for inaccuracies if you're criticizing yourself or feeling like you have no future. Irrational or pessimistic beliefs that aren't grounded in reality or facts are referred to as distorted thinking.

Asking yourself "Are these valid, truly accurate, or fair?" will help you combat negative beliefs. Try to imagine how you would react if a buddy confided in you these ideas. You may be able to see things more clearly if you journal.

Laugh out loud

Studies show that laughing might help people feel less stressed and depressed. According to studies, laughing reduces the stress hormones cortisol and adrenaline in your body. Additionally, it may increase mood-enhancing substances like dopamine and serotonin.

Keep a notebook of appreciation

Write down things you're thankful for on days when you're feeling especially sad. According to research, cultivating appreciation is associated with decreased levels of depression. You may focus on the things, no matter how tiny, that give your life purpose by expressing thankfulness.

Keep a notebook nearby on your coffee table or bedside. Focus on your positive emotions by thinking about the people or situations that make you feel good. Then, record them. Every day, try to write down five things for which you are thankful.

Motivate others

Turning your focus to someone else is one strategy for lifting a gloomy mood. According to studies, expressing support for others by saying "you" instead of "I" might help you control your own emotions.How does this appear? Try saying something straightforward to a store worker, such as "Thank you, you are always so helpful." Or ask a buddy who is through a difficult period, "What do you need?"

Use meditation or mindfulness techniques

When you're feeling down, mindfulness might be a useful technique. It can assist in shifting your attention away from your depressive symptoms and in bringing in some curiosity and possibly even hope.

You could feel better as a result of engaging in meditation activities, particularly those that help you stop worrying and ruminating. Don't wait till you're feeling down, advises Purcell. Instead, develop the practice of sitting in silence first thing in the morning.

CHAPTER FIVE: LIFESTYLE CHANGES

Exercise and Depression

One major psychological advantage of frequent physical activity is increased self-esteem. Your body produces endorphin-related compounds when you exercise.

These endorphins interact with the brain's pain-relieving receptors to lessen your experience of discomfort. Similar to morphine, endorphins cause a good feeling to arise in the body.

For instance, the sensation after a run or workout is frequently referred to as "euphoric." That sensation, referred to as a "runner's high," might be accompanied by a vivacious and invigorating view on life. By acting as analgesics, endorphins reduce the sense of pain.

They also have sedative effects. In reaction to brain chemicals known as neurotransmitters, they are produced in your brain, spinal cord, and several other areas of your body. Endorphins link to the same neuron receptors that certain painkillers connect to. The body's endorphins activate these receptors, but unlike morphine, they do not cause addiction or dependency. Depression may be successfully treated with exercise, according to research.

Serotonin and norepinephrine, neurotransmitters linked to emotions of pleasure and wellbeing, can both be elevated by exercise.

Exercise has been shown to enhance mood, sleep, energy levels, and weariness in addition to its mood-boosting benefits. Additionally, it can aid in boosting self-confidence and lessening social isolation, two typical indicators of sadness.

Exercise comes in a variety of forms and can be helpful in controlling depression. Running, swimming, or cycling are examples of aerobic exercises that have been demonstrated to be particularly beneficial in elevating mood and easing depressive symptoms.

Exercises involving body weight or resistance training, such as lifting weights, can also be useful in easing the symptoms of depression.

It's crucial to start out softly and gradually build up your workout time and intensity over time. Finding an exercise program that you like and works into your schedule is also crucial. This may improve adherence and motivation to the workout routine. To control the symptoms of depression, a healthy lifestyle must be maintained in addition to routine exercise. This includes maintaining a balanced diet, obtaining enough rest, and abstaining from drugs and alcohol. In conclusion, exercise can be a successful depression therapy.

Regular exercise can help elevate mood, lessen depressive symptoms, and boost emotions of wellbeing. To treat the symptoms of depression, it's critical to start out cautiously, establish an exercise program you love, and keep up a healthy lifestyle.

Nutrition and Depression

Generally speaking, diet is crucial for both preventing and treating depression. A balanced diet rich in complex carbs, lean protein, probiotics, and a range of fruits and vegetables might help elevate mood and lessen depressive symptoms.

Additionally, because they might exacerbate the symptoms of depression, processed foods, and alcohol should be avoided. People with depression can benefit greatly from certain meals, such as:

Fruits and vegetables are full of vitamins, minerals, and antioxidants that can help lower inflammation and elevate mood. Citrus fruits, berries, and leafy greens are just a few examples of foods strong in vitamin C that have been demonstrated to be particularly beneficial for easing the symptoms of depression.

Complex carbs: Complex carbohydrates, which are abundant in whole grains, beans, and lentils, can help control blood sugar levels and elevate mood. It has been demonstrated that high-fiber diets, in particular oatmeal, brown rice, and quinoa, are particularly beneficial for easing the symptoms of depression.

Omega-3 fatty acids: These fats are abundant in foods like fatty fish, flaxseeds, and walnuts and can help lower inflammation and elevate mood. Eicosapentaenoic acid (EPA)-rich foods, such as salmon, sardines, and mackerel, in particular, have been demonstrated to be particularly beneficial for easing the symptoms of depression.

Lean protein: Lean protein, which is abundant in foods like chicken, turkey, and tofu, can help control blood sugar levels and elevate mood. Tryptophan-rich foods, such as turkey, poultry, and eggs, have been demonstrated to be particularly beneficial for easing the symptoms of sadness.

Probiotics: Yogurt, kefir, and kimchi are full of probiotics, which can enhance gut health and lessen depressive symptoms. According to research, there is a direct link between gut health and mental health, and enhancing gut health can help lessen depressive symptoms.

The following foods can exacerbate the symptoms of depression:

Processed food: This kind of food contains a lot of sugar, salt, and bad fats. Blood sugar levels may jump and then plummet as a result of them, resulting in weariness and mood fluctuations. Inflammation in the body, which has been connected to depression, may also be brought on by them.

Fast food: Fast food frequently has a lot of calories, bad fats, and salt. Overindulging in fast food can result in weight gain and other health issues, both of which can heighten feelings of despair.

Alcohol: Alcohol is depressive, therefore it can make depression symptoms worse. Additionally, it may disrupt sleep, which exacerbates sadness.

Caffeine: Although it might temporarily improve your energy, caffeine can also disrupt your sleep and make you anxious. Dehydration from consuming too much coffee might make depression symptoms worse.

Refined carbs: Consuming refined carbohydrates, such as white bread, pasta, and rice, can trigger mood swings and weariness by causing blood sugar levels to jump and then plummet. Inflammation in the body, which has been connected to depression, may also be brought on by them.

Dairy goods that are high in fat: Dairy products that are rich in fat, such as cheese and butter, might contain a lot of harmful fats. Consuming these items in excess might result in weight gain and other health issues, which can worsen depression.

Sleep and Depression

Sleep and depression are intimately related. Most depressed individuals have trouble sleeping. In fact, if patients are not complaining of sleep problems, clinicians may be hesitant to identify depression.

Sleep problems and depression are mutually related. In other words, having depression increases the likelihood that a person may have sleep issues, and having bad sleep can contribute to the development of depression. It might be difficult to determine whether sleep problems or depression began initially because of their intricate relationship.

How to Sleep Better When Depressed

Sleep disorders can raise the likelihood of depression initially forming, as well as the risk of relapsing in those who have successfully undergone treatment for depression. Implementing these healthy behaviors will thus improve your mood, help you sleep better, and lessen some of the difficult symptoms of depression.

Consult a therapist

You may improve your sleep-related thinking patterns and manage depression using a variety of therapeutic modalities. You can get support from therapeutic approaches like CBT, interpersonal psychotherapy, and psychodynamic therapy to work with some of the underlying emotions and difficulties that cause depression. Professionals in the field of mental health can also provide specific behavioral recommendations to lessen some of the symptoms of depression and offer coping methods to deal with restless, sleepless nights.

Maintain a Regular Sleep Schedule

Having depression might make it challenging to maintain a routine. Your body has a chance to obtain at least seven hours of sleep each night if you wake up and go to bed at the same time every day. Creating a nighttime routine also serves as a cue for the body to relax and get ready for sleep.

A careful nap

It may be tempting to take a nap during the day if you have trouble sleeping at night or have unpredictable sleep patterns, but it's vital to keep naps brief. According to research, a nap should last between 10 and 20 minutes, or what is known as a "power nap." Power naps can improve performance by reducing tiredness, regulating emotions, and managing fatigue. While naps less than 10 minutes are insufficient to get the advantages of sleeping, naps longer than 20 minutes may hinder your ability to fall asleep.

Skip the alcohol

It might be tempting to take a few drinks to help you unwind and go to sleep, but alcohol is bad for sleep. Even moderate drinking can interrupt the sleep cycle and reduce REM sleep, despite research showing that binge drinking before bed makes it harder to fall asleep and remain asleep.

Move outside.

One of the simplest strategies to help your sleep if you have depression is to spend time outside. The body's internal clock and circadian rhythms are brought into harmony by exposure to sunshine, providing signals for when to be up and when to sleep.

For instance, exposure to sunshine on a regular basis sends a message to the body to stay aware and active. The body then creates melatonin when the sun sets to encourage sleep and increase drowsiness. Spending time outside can be a quick and efficient approach to activate the brain's natural chemicals that support restful sleep.

Exercise consistently

According to research, those who exercise lightly, moderately, or vigorously report having very good or decent sleep. Additionally, consistent exercise has been demonstrated to considerably lessen depressive symptoms, making it a fantastic alternative for enhancing both mental and sleep health. If you decide to start an exercise routine, think about doing it in the morning as exercising in the evening could make it difficult for you to get to sleep.

Substance Abuse and Depression

People who are struggling with drug or alcohol addiction are frequently depressed. Abuse of drugs or alcohol can cause or exacerbate depressive symptoms including loneliness, despair, and hopelessness.

While most individuals go through ups and downs in life, severe depression can endure for weeks, months, or even years. It affects all aspects of a person's life, including their capacity to work and lead healthy lives. Sometimes using drugs and alcohol might seem like a simple fix for individuals who are depressed and believe there is no end in sight.

These drugs might make you feel happier and temporarily relieve any emotional suffering. These drugs can, however, develop an addiction. Your body will get more dependent on their effects as you take more of them. Substance usage over time can worsen depressive symptoms as well as result in long-term health issues like brain damage.

Depression and substance misuse are frequently closely related. To deal with their symptoms, many people who battle with depression resort to drugs or alcohol. Unfortunately, this can create a vicious cycle in which drug use worsens depression and depression worsens drug usage. Substance addiction and depression may be related in the following ways:

Self-medication: Those who are depressed may use alcohol or drugs as a kind of self-medication. These drugs may be used by them to dull their feelings or as a means of escape. Unfortunately, this might eventually result in addiction and exacerbate sadness.

Chemical imbalances: Abusing substances can cause chemical imbalances in the brain, which can exacerbate depressive symptoms. For instance, substances like cocaine and methamphetamine can increase dopamine levels, which can result in euphoric experiences. When the benefits fade, the brain is left with low amounts of dopamine, which can result in depressive and anxious sensations.

Social isolation: Addiction to substances can result in social isolation, which can exacerbate depressive symptoms. People who abuse alcohol or drugs may isolate themselves from friends and family, which can result in feelings of desolation and loneliness.

Co-occurring disorders: Depression is a common mental health condition that co-occurs with drug addiction in many persons. Both of these problems may worsen as a result of the other.

Withdrawal: People who attempt to stop using drugs or alcohol may have withdrawal symptoms, which may include depressive and anxious thoughts. Even if they want to, this makes it challenging for people to stop taking these substances.

CHAPTER SIX: BUILDING RESILIENCE

Developing Resilience

Although it might be difficult, building resilience when depressed is crucial to recovery. Here are some pointers for developing resilience:

Engage in Self-Care

Eat healthily, get enough sleep, and exercise frequently to meet your physical and emotional demands. Take part in enjoyable and relaxing activities. Building resilience when dealing with depression requires engaging in self-care. It's simple to overlook your physical and emotional requirements while you're unhappy, which can make it more difficult to deal with the difficulties of depression.

You can give your body and mind the tools they need to handle stress and triumph over adversity by taking care of yourself. Self-care may take many different forms, such as eating healthily, getting adequate sleep, and partaking in enjoyable and relaxing activities.

Your capacity to deal with depression may be enhanced if you engage in these routines since they can help you feel more energized, focused, and cheerful. Self-compassion, a crucial aspect of resilience, may be acquired through practicing self-care.

Being nice and sympathetic to yourself will make it easier for you to overcome obstacles and failures. Additionally, you're more prone to ask for assistance when you do, which might be a crucial component of rehabilitation. In general, taking care of oneself is crucial to developing resilience while depressed. By looking for yourself, you're giving yourself the tools you need to battle despair and triumph over challenges.

Create a Support System

Create a network of friends and relatives that can provide you with emotional support and motivation. Think about joining a support group or getting help from a professional. An essential component of developing resilience during depression is creating a support network. It's simple to believe that you are struggling alone with depression since it may be so lonely.

You may build a network of individuals who can assist you in navigating the difficulties of depression by contacting friends and family members who can provide emotional support and encouragement. A support network may offer a sympathetic ear, helpful counsel, and a sense of connection and community. Your capacity to deal with depression may increase as a result of feeling more supported and less alone.

In addition to your friends and family, you could think about joining a support group or getting treatment from a professional. A sense of community and a secure setting to express your experiences and feelings may be found in support groups.

You can get the skills and strategies you need to manage depression and develop resilience through professional assistance, such as therapy or counseling. In general, creating a support network is crucial to developing resilience throughout the depression. By asking for assistance and support, you build a network of individuals who can guide you through the difficulties of depression and help you triumph over adversity.

Practice Mindfulness

Use mindfulness practices to help you stay focused and present at the moment, such as meditation and deep breathing. You can control your anxiety and sadness with the use of this. Developing resilience when dealing with depression requires engaging in mindfulness practices.

The practice of mindfulness is being in the present and uncritically observing your thoughts, feelings, and sensations. You may manage stress and break bad thinking patterns by engaging in mindfulness practices that help you become more conscious of your thoughts and feelings.

Rumination and negative self-talk are traits of depression that can make it more difficult to deal with obstacles and failures. You may become more conscious of these tendencies and learn to stop them before they get out of hand by engaging in mindfulness practices. Additionally, mindfulness can aid in the growth of self-compassion, a crucial aspect of resilience. Being nice and sympathetic to yourself will make it easier for you to overcome obstacles and failures.

Additionally, you're more prone to ask for assistance when you do, which might be a crucial component of rehabilitation. Overall, developing resilience during depression requires engaging in mindfulness practices. You may learn to handle stress, break bad thinking patterns, and increase your sense of self-compassion by being more conscious of your thoughts and feelings.

Set objectives

A sense of direction and purpose can be provided by setting reasonable objectives. Divide more ambitious ambitions into manageable, smaller steps. Setting objectives is crucial to developing resilience while dealing with depression.

It may be challenging to feel inspired or to discover what your life is all about if you're depressed. Setting objectives can give you a sense of direction and purpose that can help you get over depressive and hopeless moods. It's crucial to be explicit, quantifiable, realistic, relevant, and time-bound while making objectives.

When you accomplish your goals, this can make you feel accomplished and can keep you motivated and focused. You may get a sense of control over your life by setting objectives.

Setting objectives allows you to actively participate in your rehabilitation even though depression can make you feel like you are at the whim of your feelings. Setting objectives is, in general, a crucial component of developing resilience during the depression. You may get rid of feelings of helplessness and despair, gain control over your life, and feel a sense of satisfaction when you accomplish your goals by developing a sense of purpose and direction.

Concentrate on your strengths

Recognize your strengths and concentrate on utilizing them to get beyond obstacles. Any achievement is worth recognizing, no matter how modest. Building resilience when dealing with depression requires you to pay attention to your strengths. Depression can leave you feeling useless and powerless and make it difficult for you to recognize your abilities and successes.

You may increase your sense of self-worth and confidence by concentrating on your strengths, which can aid you in overcoming emotions of hopelessness and despair. Finding your unique talents and values is one method to concentrate on them.

You may be able to find areas where you may have a good influence on both your own life and the lives of others, as well as build a stronger sense of purpose and direction, with the aid of this. Practice thankfulness as another strategy for concentrating on your advantages. You may divert your attention from negative thoughts and feelings and cultivate a more optimistic attitude toward life by concentrating on the good things in your life. In general, concentrating on your strengths is a crucial component of developing resilience when experiencing depression. You may overcome emotions of hopelessness and despair and cultivate a more optimistic attitude in life by growing in self-worth and confidence.

Practice Gratitude

By concentrating on the good things in your life, you might develop a sense of thankfulness. Keep a gratitude notebook or set out some time every day to think about what you have to be grateful for.

Building resilience throughout depression requires regular thankfulness practice. Depression may leave you feeling hopeless and powerless and make it difficult for you to see the good things in your life. By cultivating an attitude of appreciation, you may redirect your attention from unfavorable emotions and ideas and create a more upbeat approach to life.

Keeping a gratitude notebook is one method to cultivate thankfulness. This entails listing three things each day for which you are grateful. This can take the form of anything, from a strong cup of coffee to a helpful friend or relative.

You may increase your sense of appreciation and your sense of pleasure and well-being by concentrating on the good things in your life. Expressing your thankfulness to others is another approach to cultivating gratitude. This might be expressing gratitude for anything someone did for you or just letting someone know how much you value them. You may make your connections stronger and feel more connected and supported by showing them your thanks. In general, cultivating thankfulness is a crucial component of overcoming depression.

You may create a more optimistic attitude toward life and feel happier and more content by turning your attention away from unpleasant ideas and emotions.

Keep in mind that developing resilience requires patience and work. Be kind to yourself and acknowledge your advancements as you go.

Building Mental Toughness

Building resilience throughout depression requires developing mental toughness. Building the abilities and mentality required to triumph over adversity and accomplish your objectives despite obstacles and disappointments is a key component of building mental toughness. Having a growth mentality is one technique to combat depression and improve mental resilience.

This entails considering difficulties and failures as chances for development and education rather than as impediments to be avoided. You can improve your resilience and your ability to face problems with a positive and proactive attitude by adopting a growth mindset. Self-care is another strategy for developing mental fortitude when suffering from depression.

This entails caring for your physical, emotional, and mental well-being as well as scheduling time for interests and pursuits that make you happy and fulfilled. You may improve your sense of well-being and handle the stress and difficulties of depression by giving self-care a higher priority. Moreover, creating a support network is crucial for enhancing mental fortitude during depression. You may grow a stronger feeling of connection and support by doing this, which may entail asking friends, family, or mental health experts for support. You may better manage the difficulties of depression and increase your resilience and mental toughness by creating a support network. All things considered, developing mental toughness is a crucial component of developing resilience throughout the depression.

Even when faced with obstacles and disappointments, you can overcome adversity and accomplish your goals by cultivating a growth mindset, engaging in self-care, and creating a network of supportive people.

CHAPTER SEVEN: THE POWER OF CONNECTION

Building Relationships

Even though developing a relationship while suffering from depression might be difficult, it is doable with the appropriate attitude and strategy. Being upfront and honest with your spouse about your depression is a crucial first step.

This might entail opening up about how you're feeling, what you've gone through, and the difficulties you've had with depression. You can then collaborate to come up with coping mechanisms and solidify a solid, encouraging connection. Setting self-care and mental health as a priority is a crucial additional step.

This might entail getting support from a professional, practicing self-care techniques like meditation and exercise, and managing stress and anxiety. You may better handle the difficulties of depression and create a stronger, more resilient relationship by giving your mental health a high priority.

Building a relationship while battling depression also requires open communication. This might entail discussing your wants and boundaries with your spouse and coming up with conflict-resolution techniques as a team. This will help you construct a solid, dependable connection.

You may create a stronger, more durable connection that can withstand the difficulties of depression by speaking honestly and freely with one another. Overall, developing a relationship while battling depression might be difficult, but it is doable with the appropriate attitude and strategy.

You may create a strong, supportive relationship that can withstand the difficulties of depression by being open and honest with your spouse, placing a high priority on self-care and mental health, and communicating honestly. Without the proper response, depression may damage close relationships and leave both parties feeling estranged. Don't allow depression to deprive you of one of the most crucial things that can combat depression: a partner's support.

Be honest with your thoughts and emotions.
Your spouse won't comprehend what you're going through if you're feeling down or distant and don't express how you're feeling. Gather the courage to sit down with your

spouse and discuss your feelings in depth. Even though it may be difficult, having an honest conversation about depression is crucial for your relationship and will help you get along better.

Keep up your fitness activities

You may perform better, feel better about yourself, and feel healthier by exercising. A simple approach to being active, enjoying some sunshine, and spending time with each other is to go on walks together.

Be grateful

It's typical for sad people to withdraw indoors. Your partner can feel left out and disregarded as a result. Even if you don't feel like chatting much, letting your spouse know occasionally that they are still important to you just requires a small amount of effort. Use gestures to demonstrate your devotion if you find it difficult to concentrate or put your feelings into words.

Simple gestures like holding hands, cuddling, or giving your lover a little touch on the back can be effective methods to show your relationship that you care. These behaviors not only strengthen your relationship with your spouse, but they also produce chemicals in your brain that can lift your spirits.

Helping out when you can

Even though it may seem unimportant, helping out around the house may be a good way to let your spouse know you care. Helping out around the house, whether it's with the washing, dishes, or food prep, frees up extra time for the two of you to spend together.

Maintain interests

Being spontaneous helps keep a relationship interesting, but it might be difficult to be spontaneous when you're miserable. Instead of waiting for something pleasant to happen on its own, make plans for it (such as going out to dinner or the movies). In this manner, spending quality time with your spouse gives you something to look forward to.

Contact your partner to check in

Depression can make situations appear worse than they are. Ask your spouse how things are going from their viewpoint if you sense that anything in your relationship isn't quite right. When you're depressed, you often interpret events harsher than they are.

Make yourself available

Make oneself open for discussion, even if it is only about routine daily issues. Even if you don't want to chat as much, pay attention to what your spouse is saying since we all admire good listeners.

Finding Support Systems

It is crucial to get help while dealing with depression. You require a network of supportive individuals, including close relatives, friends, coworkers, and neighbors who enable you to be who you are.

A crucial component of a self-care strategy is creating and maintaining a strong support network of individuals who can offer encouragement, assist you in continuing to move and engage in meaningful activities, and assist you in challenging your negative thinking. You gain from having a network of dependable connections in the following ways:

Better mental and physical wellness. Support networks help preserve both physical and mental health. We may stay active and partake in important activities with the aid of our connections. Additionally, it might enhance our emotional health. These advantages, according to researchers, result from a combination of reduced stress and greater brain activity.

Enhanced sense of security and belonging. Spending time with others and realizing you're not alone helps to lessen feelings of loneliness. It might be reassuring to know that you have friends to turn to in difficult times. Joining a support group or conversing with people who have dealt with depression might show you that you're not alone and that there are solutions to overcome depression.

Superiority in problem-solving. Your social support system can assist you in problem-solving and stress reduction. There's a good chance that others are going through similar things, and they might be able to provide you with some helpful pointers, counsel, or methods that they've found to work.

Accountability. Making successful lifestyle changes has been found to depend heavily on having someone else hold you accountable. When someone else is working toward their objectives as well, accountability is most effective; in addition to reporting your success to someone else, let that person be accountable to you for the goals they've set for themselves.

Creating Your Support System

Several suggestions for creating your support network include:

Volunteer. Choose a cause that matters to you and get engaged; give some of your time to a local charity or house of worship. Volunteering will put you in contact with others who share your interests and beliefs and will offer you the satisfaction of doing action to further your principles.

Adopt a sport or sign up for a gym. Your mental and physical health will benefit from this, and you may have the chance to make some new friends as well.

Create a book club and ask some new acquaintances to participate. Making new acquaintances is a lot of fun when you talk about fascinating topics and exchange ideas and views.

Get to know your coworkers and neighbors. Try to get to know some of the acquaintances you run into frequently.

Join groups for professionals. Not only will taking this action benefit your future job, but it will also allow you to expand your social network to include others in your industry. Friends in the same line of work might sometimes relate to your difficulties more than anyone else.

Make use of the internet. Social networking websites may aid in maintaining relationships with friends and family. Several websites can offer specific help if you are going through trying times or altering circumstances, including becoming a parent for the first time, dealing with a loved one's life-threatening sickness, or experiencing some other difficulty. When setting up meetings with somebody you have only met online, be careful to stay with trustworthy sites and exercise common sense.

Joining Support Groups

A powerful strategy to manage depression and create a strong support network is to join a support group. Individuals can connect with others who are going through similar situations, express their thoughts and concerns, and get emotional support and direction in a safe and supportive atmosphere provided through support groups.

The ability to feel less alone and lonely is one advantage of attending a support group. People can feel more connected and supported, as well as more understood and validated, by interacting with others who are experiencing similar things.

A further advantage of attending a support group is that it may provide people with useful skills and methods for managing depression. Support groups may provide people with informational materials, coping mechanisms, and other tools that might help them manage their symptoms and develop resilience.

Additionally, being a part of a support group may provide people with a feeling of direction and significance in their life. People can increase their empathy and compassion as well as their motivation to make positive changes in their life by connecting with others who are experiencing similar things.

Overall, being a part of a support group may help you manage your depression and develop a solid network of friends. People may increase their resilience and enhance their general well-being by connecting with others who are going through similar situations, getting emotional support and counseling, and learning useful techniques for managing depression.

Joining a support group is a good method for people with depression to connect with others who are experiencing the same things they are, get emotional support from them, and get advice.

These actions can assist people in locating a support group that is ideal for them:

Speak with a healthcare professional: For those looking for support groups, healthcare professionals may be an invaluable resource. They might be able to suggest nearby support groups or provide you with details on online support groups.

Conduct an internet search: Finding local or online support groups can be facilitated by conducting an online search. Local support group listings may be found on websites and internet discussion boards can help people connect with others who are going through comparable circumstances.

Speak with local mental health organizations: These organizations may be able to tell you about local support groups or offer support groups themselves. The National Alliance on Mental Illness (NAMI), Mental Health America, and regional community mental health centers are a few examples of these organizations.

Consult with friends and family members: These people may be aware of local support organizations or be able to offer their assistance.

Attend a support group meeting: Going to a meeting of a support group might be a good opportunity to find out more about the group and see if it's a good match. Numerous support organizations welcome new members and offer free or inexpensive sessions.

In general, joining a support group may be a helpful method for people who are struggling with depression to connect with others who are experiencing comparable things and receive emotional support and advice.

Helping Others

Especially while struggling with depression, helping others may be a potent approach to enhance your mental health and well-being. The following are some ways that assisting others might lessen depression:

Increases self-esteem:. Helping others makes you feel good about yourself and the difference you are making in the lives of others. You may feel more assured and capable as a result of this sense of accomplishment and purpose, which may boost your self-esteem. Helping others may also result in good feedback and recognition, which may make you feel better about yourself.

Last but not least, giving to others will help you divert your attention from your issues and concerns, which will make you feel happier and more hopeful about your own life. Overall, when battling depression, giving to others may be a potent approach to enhance self-esteem.

Gives a sense of purpose: Helping others may give you a reason to get out of bed in the morning and a sense of meaning and satisfaction in your life, which can give you a sense of purpose when you're feeling down. You feel as though you are changing the world and adding to something greater than yourself when you assist others.

This sense of purpose may increase your motivation and vigor and can give you a cause to persist even in the face of challenges. Furthermore, when you serve others, you could uncover new hobbies and passions that can give your life meaning and direction. In general, while suffering from depression, helping others may be a potent approach to give one a feeling of purpose.

Strengthens social connections: By giving people the chance to socialize and establish new contacts, helping others can help people who are depressed strengthen their social connections. When you serve others, you frequently collaborate with others to achieve a similar objective, which may foster a feeling of connection and camaraderie.

In addition, helping others may introduce you to new individuals who share your interests and beliefs, which can facilitate the development of new friendships and social ties. Finally, helping others may result in gratitude and praise from the people you are helping, which may increase your sense of worth and community. In general, when battling depression, assisting others can be a potent approach to strengthening social ties.

Reduces stress: Helping others may alleviate stress when you're sad by giving your life meaning and purpose, which can make you feel more in control and less overwhelmed. Helping others forces you to put your attention on other people's needs, which might help you turn your attention away from your issues and concerns. Your outlook on your own life will improve as a result, which will assist to lessen tension and worry.

Additionally, when you help others, you could get compliments and praise. These things can make you feel more competent and confident, which will help you feel less stressed. Finally, by helping others, you may create a network of individuals who are concerned about you and wish to assist you in times of need. This network can act as a potent stress-relieving buffer. Overall, volunteering may be a great approach to relieve stress when battling depression.

Improves physical health: By lowering stress and fostering happy emotions, helping others can enhance physical health when you're depressed. These pleasant feelings can then have a favorable effect on your physical health. Helping others involves a lot of physical exercises, such as working at a food bank or sprucing up a park, which may keep you fit and active. Additionally, when you assist others, you could get a feeling of meaning and purpose in your life. This may increase your motivation to look after your physical health.

Finally, helping others may help you develop social ties and a support system of people who are concerned about you and want to keep you well, which can be a strong incentive to take good care of your physical health. Overall, while battling depression, assisting others may be a strong strategy to enhance physical wellness.

Increases happy emotions: By giving you a feeling of direction and significance in your life, which might lift your spirits when you're melancholy. Helping others forces you to put your attention on other people's needs, which might help you turn your attention away from your issues and concerns. This can promote happy feelings by making you feel more upbeat and hopeful about your own life. Additionally, when you help others, you could get praise and recognition. These things might make you feel more competent and self-assured, which will further boost your pleasant emotions.

Additionally, by helping others, you may develop a network of friends and family members who will be there for you in times of need. These relationships and networks can be a strong source of happy feelings. Overall, when suffering from depression, helping others may be a strong strategy to promote happy feelings.

In general, lending a hand to others may be a potent approach to enhance your mental health and well-being, particularly if you're struggling with depression. Helping others can help relieve depression and enhance your overall quality of life by raising self-esteem, giving a sense of purpose, developing social connections, lowering stress, enhancing physical health, and promoting happy emotions.

CHAPTER EIGHT: MOVING FORWARD

Fighting the Shame and Silence of Depression

Many people who battle with depression may feel ashamed or embarrassed about their disease. Depression can be a tough and solitary experience. It may be challenging to ask for support and assistance, and it may be challenging to recover from depression as a result of this shame and silence.

But it is crucial to keep in mind that depression is a common and curable disorder and that asking for help is a show of strength rather than weakness. Talking about your experience with dependable friends, family members, or mental health experts is one of the most crucial things you can do to combat the guilt and silence that come with depression. Sharing your thoughts and feelings with others might make you feel less isolated and provide you with the support and inspiration you need to get through a depressive episode.

Talking honestly about your sadness can also lessen the shame and stigma attached to mental illness, which may make it simpler for other people to get care. Learning more about the problem and the many available treatments is a crucial first step in overcoming the guilt and silence that come with having depression. Understanding that depression is a medical issue and not a sign of personal weakness might help you feel better.

There are also excellent therapies available. You may feel more in control and less embarrassed to ask for assistance as a result of this understanding. Last, but not least, it's critical to keep in mind that recovering from depression is a process and that feeling better may require time and work.

Be kind to yourself and don't be embarrassed to ask for assistance when you require it. Be mindful of the fact that you are not alone and that many individuals have overcome depression. You can beat depression and have a happy, healthy life with the correct support and care.

Ending the Stigma of Depression

Even though depression is a common and curable disorder, many sufferers may experience stigma or shame as a result of their condition. This stigma might make it challenging to ask for support and assistance as well as to recover from depression. But it is possible to eradicate the stigma associated with depression and build a culture that is more accepting and understanding. Educating others about the disorder and its repercussions is one of the most crucial stages in eradicating the stigma associated with depression.

Sharing knowledge about depression's symptoms, the many forms of therapy available, and the significance of getting assistance when you need it may all fall under this category. We can work to lessen the stigma attached to mental illness and encourage more people to get the treatment they need by raising awareness and understanding of depression.

Contesting inaccurate preconceptions and preconceived notions about mental illness is a crucial step in the effort to eradicate the stigma of depression. This might involve advocating for more uplifting and kind messaging about mental health as well as speaking out against damaging language and attitudes.

We can contribute to the development of a more accepting and inclusive society for persons who suffer from depression and other mental health issues by combating stigma and fostering understanding. Finally, it's critical to keep in mind that sadness can be recovered from and that getting treatment is a show of strength, not weakness.

We can lessen the shame and stigma attached to depression and other mental health issues by sharing success stories and spreading messages of hope and resiliency. Together, we can fight to eradicate the stigma associated with depression and build a society that is more forgiving and encouraging of all people.

Advocating for Mental Health

People who labor diligently every day to tell their stories and assist others in need who do not wear capes are heroes who advocate for mental health. By speaking the truth, they take chances and display their vulnerabilities in the hopes of inspiring someone else.

These champions speak up for those without a voice, whether it be through a blog, social media, book, or public speech. We are reminded by them that we are not alone in facing challenges.

They serve as a reminder that we are innocent. They serve as a reminder that this path is filled with light, healing, and hope. They dispel stigma and preconceived notions about mental illness. It might be difficult to promote mental wellness, especially if you are experiencing despair.

But it's crucial to keep in mind that talking about mental health may lessen the stigma attached to it and make others feel less isolated in their challenges. Here are some pointers for supporting mental health advocacy:

Begin small

You don't have to post your darkest, most intimate secrets on social media to support a cause. By discreetly discussing your experiences with depression with a friend, neighbor, or family member, you may speak out for others and urge them to get assistance if they need it.

A mental health organization or social media allows you to share your story anonymously. To promote mental health, you don't need to be a public speaker or a social media celebrity. If you're not ready, you aren't obligated to tell your tale either.

Locate a welcoming neighborhood

Connecting with people who are going through similar situations might be made possible by joining a support group for mental health or an online community. These groups can give you a safe place to talk about your experiences and promote mental wellness.

Continue to learn

Being more knowledgeable about mental health and mental illness may make you a more powerful advocate. Learn more about mental health and how to help individuals who are struggling by reading books, going to seminars, and listening to podcasts.

Speak aloud

Use your voice to promote mental health, whether it be on social media, via a blog post, or when speaking at an event. Tell your experience, advocate for mental health services, and dispel myths and misconceptions about mental illness.

Look out for yourself

It may be emotionally taxing to promote mental health, particularly if you are depressed. Be careful to look after yourself by engaging in self-care, getting help when you require it, and taking breaks as required.

Remember, promoting mental health is a crucial component of eliminating stigma and increasing awareness of mental illness. You may change the lives of those who are dealing with mental health difficulties by sharing your stories and encouraging others to get assistance.

YOU ARE ENOUGH

www.ingramcontent.com/pod-product-compliance
Lightning Source LLC
Chambersburg PA
CBHW070902260726
48661CB00004B/1548